Response Activities

On-Level
Grade 1

Harcourt School Publishers

www.harcourtschool.com

Response Activities

On-Level
Grade 1

⧉Harcourt School Publishers

www.harcourtschool.com

ISBN 10 0-15-362626-7

ISBN 13 978-0-15-362626-5

1 2 3 4 5 6 7 8 9 10   947   16 15 14 13 12 11 10 09 08 07

Let's Pretend!

YOU WILL NEED

- paper
- markers
- tape or glue

Are you a cat? Are you a rat?

1. Cut one big circle. Cut two small triangles.

2. Stick the triangles on the circle.

3. Draw a face.

4. A cat says *meow!* A rat says *squeak!*

Duck's Card

YOU WILL NEED
- White paper
- Pencil
- Crayons

Duck sent Dog a card to ask about her visit. Let's make Duck's card!

1 Fold a sheet of paper in half.

2 Draw and color a picture on the front of the card.

3 Write Duck's note inside the card.

Hi, Dog
I miss you.
Love,
Duck

I Like It Too!

What do you like? What do your friends like?

1 Draw a line down the middle of the paper.

2 Draw foods you like.

3 Draw animals you like.

4 Show your friends. Do they like these things, too?

At Home, at Camp

YOU WILL NEED

- paper
- pencils
- colored pencils or markers

Tell the differences between home and camp.

1. Get a piece of paper. Draw a line in the middle from top to bottom.

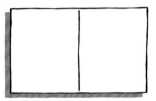

2. On the left, write Home. On the right, write Camp.

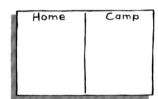

3. Draw how you eat, sleep, and play at home.

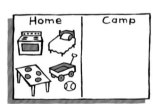

4. Draw how you eat, sleep, and play at camp.

What Will Jill Dig?

Why does Jill dig? Think big!

1 Jill digs. She makes a big hole.

2 What will Jill make? Draw it!

3 What do your friends think?

I Can Bake a Pie

YOU WILL NEED
- paper
- pencils

Write a recipe for your favorite pie.

1 Choose four ingredients for your pie.

blueberries	green grapes	orange juice	rocks
butter	grass	pink flowers	feathers
fish	milk	red apples	water

2 Tell how to make your pie.

3 Share your recipe with your friends.

blueberries
grass
butter
green grapes

grass
pink flowers
butter
rocks

Making Music

Make a shaker. Play with friends!

YOU WILL NEED

- bottles with caps
- rice, dry beans, or beads

1 Pick a bottle.

2 Put some rice, beans, or beads in the bottle. Put in a lot or a little.

3 Shake the bottle. How does it sound?

4 Play together. Make music with your friends.

Animal Helpers

YOU WILL NEED
- paper
- markers or crayons

How can you help animals?

1 Edmund and Drum help the turtles.

2 Draw how you can help animals, too.

3 Label your picture. Give it a title.

What's Next?

YOU WILL NEED

- paper
- pencil
- crayons or markers

What will happen to Jack and Mom?

1 Jack and Mom did not get a raft.

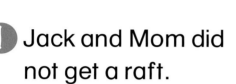

2 Write: "Jack and Mom went to Bill."

3 Tell what happens next.

4 Draw a picture to go with your story.

SAFE Song

YOU WILL NEED
- paper
- markers or crayons

Make a safety song.

1 Use a large sheet of paper. Write SAFE down the page.

2 Choose words to go in your song.

S: stop and think	A: ask a friend	F: family can help	E: everywhere you go
slow down	away from home	friends can help	each time you play
stay close	always take care	find a safe spot	everywhere you are

3 Draw pictures to go with your song.

Map It!

YOU WILL NEED

- paper
- pencil
- crayons or markers

Make a map of your classroom.

1 Draw a big rectangle on the paper. This is your classroom.

2 Draw things inside your classroom. Label them.

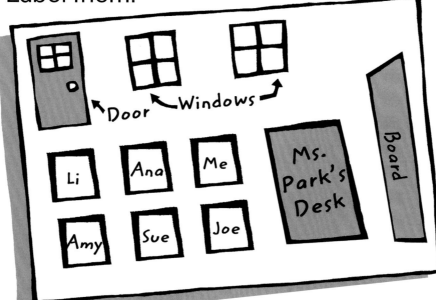

Silly Dilly Animals

Make an amazing animal!

1 Get two pieces of paper. Draw an animal on each sheet.

2 Cut your animals in half.

3 Put animal parts together to make one animal.

4 Name your silly dilly animal.

Monkabbit

 Little and BIG

YOU WILL NEED
- paper
- pencil

You are a big kid. What can you do now?

1 Fold your paper in half.

2 On one side, write "Little."
On the other side,
write "Big."

3 What can little kids do?
Write or draw these things.

4 What can big kids do?
Write or draw these things.

Animal Babies

YOU WILL NEED
- paper
- markers or crayons

Where do animal babies live?

1. Ginger was under the bed with her kittens. Kittens live in a quiet place with a mommy cat.

2. Where do bird babies live? Draw it!

3. Where do frog babies live? Draw it!

4. Where do butterfly babies live? Draw it!

Job Jar

YOU WILL NEED
- a can or box
- pencil
- paper
- scissors

Make a job jar. Help out at home or school.

1. Cut paper into strips.

2. Write a job on the paper.

Clean my room.

3. Write many jobs. Put the papers into the jar.

4. Pick a paper and do the job!

Put books away.

Liz Can Mix

My Community

YOU WILL NEED

• paper

• markers or crayons

Draw things in your community.

1 Draw your home.

2 Draw a friend's home. Draw a road from your home to your friend's home.

3 Draw where you like to play. Draw a road from your home to where you play.

4 Draw your school. Draw a road from your home to your school.

All About Puppies

This game is like *Simon Says*.

1 Choose a leader.

2 The leader says what a puppy can do. She makes a funny move.

3 If a puppy can do it, follow the leader!

4 If a puppy can't do it, stand still!

5 Take turns being leader.

6 Tell one thing a puppy can do.

A puppy can _____.

A Puppy Can't Clap

Let's Play Ball at Home

YOU WILL NEED
• paper
• pencil

Tell a story about Jess, Jean, and Walter.

1 Jess, Jean, and Walter go home to play ball. They find three balls.

2 Tell how they play with each ball.

3 Draw pictures to go with your story.

Head, Hands, Knees, and Feet

YOU WILL NEED

- a large sheet of paper
- markers

Your body is special. Draw what you can do!

1 Draw yourself.

2 Write or draw something you do with your head.

3 Write or draw something you do with your hands.

4 Write or draw something you do with your knees.

5 Write or draw something you do with your feet.

Jake's Picnic

YOU WILL NEED
- paper
- markers or crayons

Make a picnic for Jake!

1 Draw a picnic blanket.

2 What does Jake like to eat? Draw it.

3 What will Jake play with? Draw it.

4 Draw Jake at his picnic.

Grade 1, Lesson 21

Jake Runs Away

Animal Pocket Book

Choose an animal you like. Write a book about it.

1 Take two pieces of paper. Fold them both in half.

2 Put one inside the other. You made a book!

3 On the front, draw an animal you like.

4 In the book, tell about your animal:

A _____ lives in a _____.

A baby _____ is called a _____.

A _____ eats _____.

5 Share your book with friends!

Snowscapes

YOU WILL NEED

- blue and black construction paper
- cotton balls
- scissors
- glue
- chalk

Make a snow picture.

1 Use blue paper for day.
Use black paper for night.

2 Put glue where the snow will be.

3 Use a cotton ball to make snow!

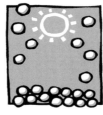 

4 Use chalk to draw!

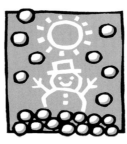 

The King's Feelings

Do a skit. Act out the king's feelings.

1 What made the king feel happy? Act it out.

2 What made the king feel mad? Act it out.

3 What made the king feel sad? Act it out.

4 Finish the sentence.

I liked when the king was _____

because _____

_____.

The **BIG** Picture

YOU WILL NEED
- paper
- markers or crayons

Water falls from the watering can. Draw the big picture!

1. Draw Stick Insect's home.

2. Draw Beetle's home next to Stick Insect's home.

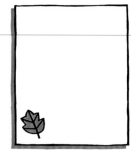

3. Draw Ant's home next to Beetle's home.

4. Draw the watering can. Make it big! Show how the water falls on the three homes.

Sense Bubbles

YOU WILL NEED

- a large sheet of paper
- pencil
- markers

Tell how you use your senses!

1 Make five big circles on your paper.

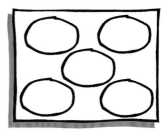

2 Put a sense in each circle.

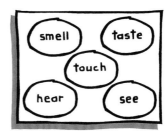

3 Read "A Kitten Grows." Find things you taste, smell, see, touch, and hear.

4 Write them in the circles with the sense they match.

touch
soft

Sand Painting

Make a picture. Paint with sand!

YOU WILL NEED

- paper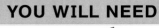
- paintbrush
- sand
- spoon
- paint

1 Paint a picture.

2 Put sand on the wet painting.

3 Let it dry.

Mark Comes Home

YOU WILL NEED
- paper
- pencil

Make a plan for Mark and Ross.

1 Number 1–5 on your page.

2 Tell the things Ross and Mark will do today.

3 Draw pictures.

TRUNK PAINTING

YOU WILL NEED

- paper
- paintbrush
- rubber band
- paint

Paint like an elephant!

1 Put a rubber band around your wrist.

2 Put the paintbrush under the rubber band.

3 Make a trunk like an elephant!

4 Try to paint a picture.

Can Animals Paint?

Author, Author!

YOU WILL NEED

- paper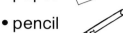
- pencil
- markers or crayons

Make a book.

1. Take two pieces of paper. Fold them both in half.

2. Make a title. Write your name. You are the author!

3. Write a story about your family. Draw pictures to go with the story.

4. Share your book with friends.

A Bird Branch

How many birds can you balance?

YOU WILL NEED

- a box of toothpicks
- glue
- clay
- tape

1. Put some clay on the table.
   Use toothpicks to make a tree trunk.

2. Use toothpicks and clay to make a tree.

3. Make birds out of clay.

4. Try to balance birds on the branches.

5. Count the birds!

Always Room for More